It's Easy To Play Showstoppers.

Les Misérables

Wise Publications
London / New York / Paris / Sydney / Copenhagen / Madrid

Exclusive Distributors:

Music Sales Limited
8/9 Frith Street, London W1V 5TZ, England.

Music Sales Pty Limited
120 Rothschild Avenue, Rosebery, NSW 2018, Australia.

Order No. AM956230
ISBN 0-7119-7913-8
This book © Copyright 1999 by Wise Publications.

Book design by Michael Bell Design.
Cover photograph courtesy of Rex Features.
Compiled by Nick Crispin.
Music arranged by Stephen Duro.
Music processed by Allegro Reproductions.

Music Sales' complete catalogue describes thousands of titles and
is available in full colour sections by subject, direct from Music Sales Limited.
Please state your areas of interest and send a cheque/postal order for £1.50 for postage to:
Music Sales Limited, Newmarket Road, Bury St. Edmunds, Suffolk IP33 3YB.

www.musicsales.co.uk

Your Guarantee of Quality:
As publishers, we strive to produce every book to the highest commercial standards.
The music has been freshly engraved and the book has been carefully designed to minimise awkward page turns and to make playing from it a real pleasure.
Particular care has been given to specifying acid-free, neutral-sized paper made from pulps which have not been elemental chlorine bleached.
This pulp is from farmed sustainable forests and was produced with special regard for the environment.
Throughout, the printing and binding have been planned to ensure a sturdy, attractive publication which should give years of enjoyment.
If your copy fails to meet our high standards, please inform us and we will gladly replace it.

Printed in the United Kingdom by
Caligraving Limited, Thetford, Norfolk.

Big Spender
(Sweet Charity)

Words by Dorothy Fields
Music by Cy Coleman

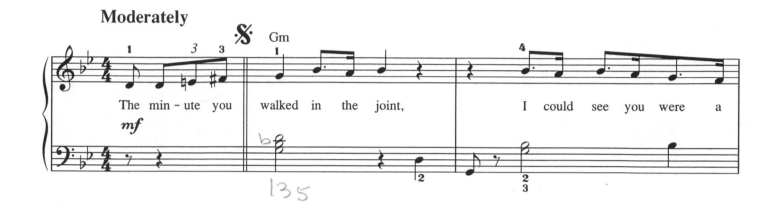

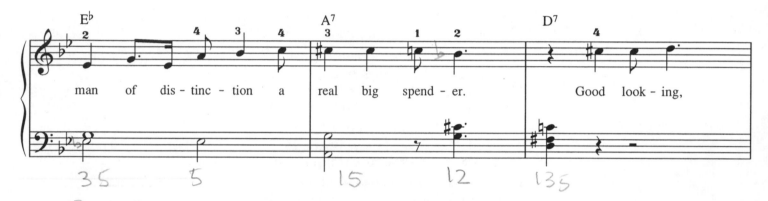

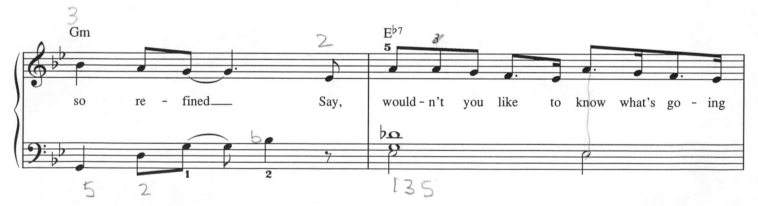

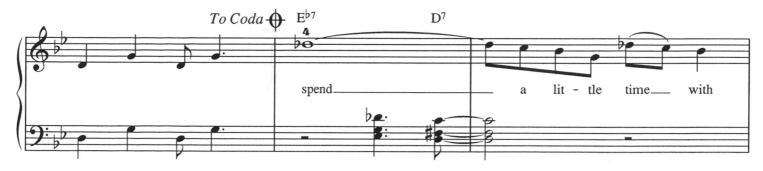

let me show you a good time.___ The min-ute you

CODA

Hey! Big Spend-er, Hey! Big Spend-er,

1245
EbF Ab Cb
5 2

spend_____ a lit-tle time___ with

135

me, spend a lit-tle time___ with me,

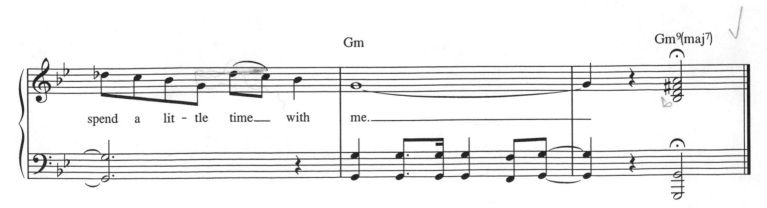

spend a lit-tle time___ with me.___

Don't Cry For Me Argentina
(Evita)

Music by Andrew Lloyd Webber
Lyrics by Tim Rice

Slowly

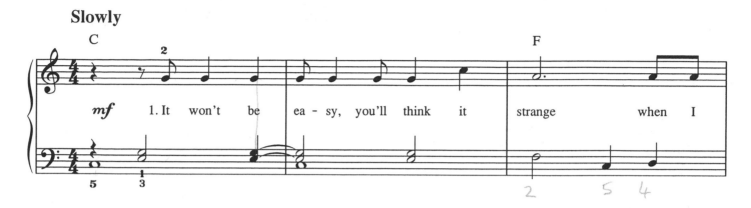

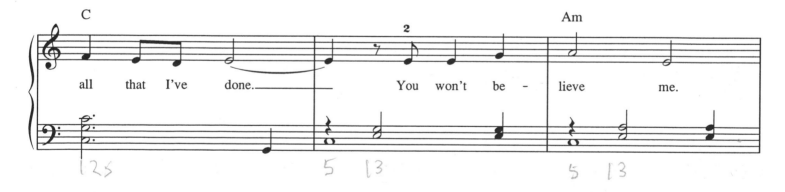

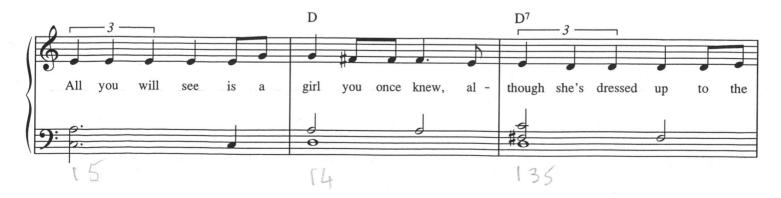

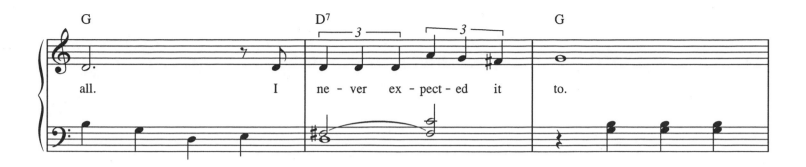

all. I ne-ver ex-pect-ed it to.

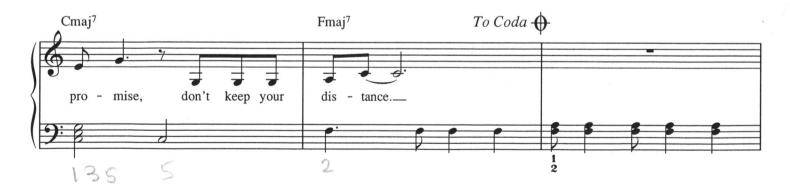

Don't cry for me, Ar-gen-ti-na, the truth is I ne-ver

left you. All through my wild days, my mad ex-is-tence, I kept my

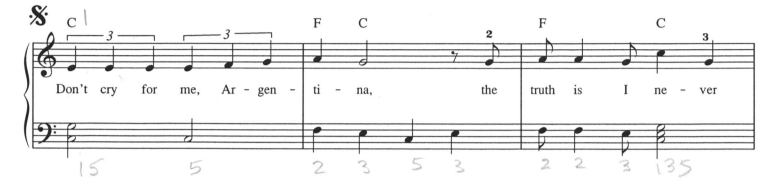

pro-mise, don't keep your dis-tance.

To Coda

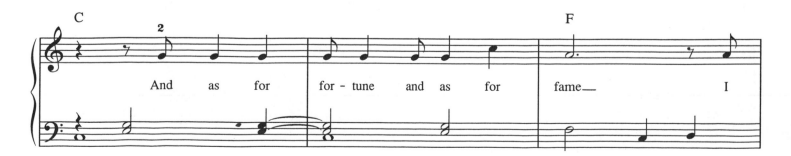

And as for for-tune and as for fame I

ne - ver   in - vi - ted them   in: Though it   seemed   to the world   they were

all   I   de - sired.   They   are   il - lu -   sions,   they're

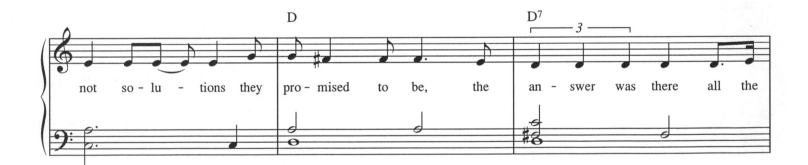

not   so - lu - tions they   pro - mised   to   be,   the   an - swer   was   there   all   the

D.S. al Coda

time   I   love you   and hope   you love   me.

CODA

Have I said too much? There's no-thing more I can think of to say to you.

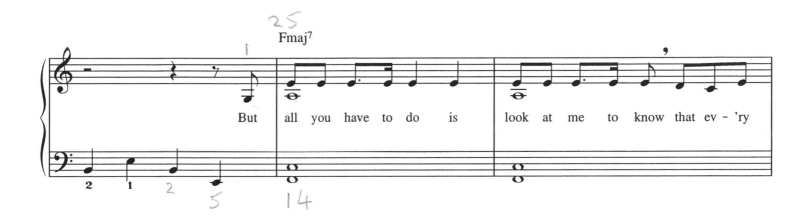

But all you have to do is look at me to know that ev-'ry

word is true.

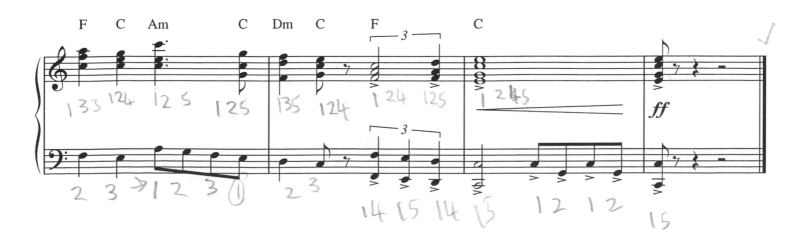

Luck Be A Lady

(Guys And Dolls)

Words & Music by Frank Loesser

Moderately bright

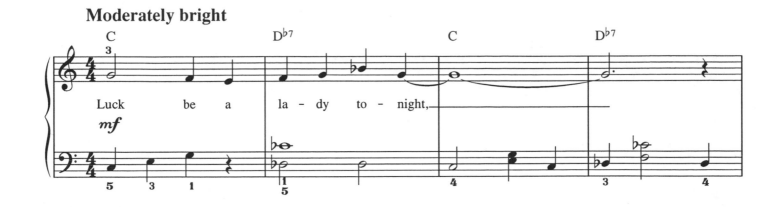

Luck be a la-dy to-night,

Luck be a la-dy to-night. Luck if you've

ev-er been a la-dy to be-gin with, luck be a

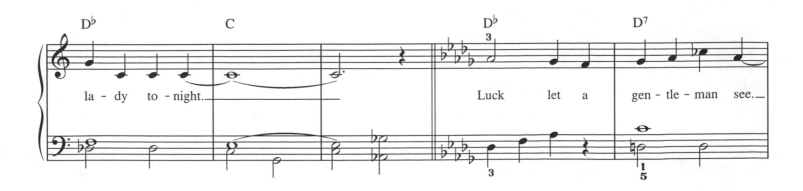

la-dy to-night. Luck let a gen-tle-man see.

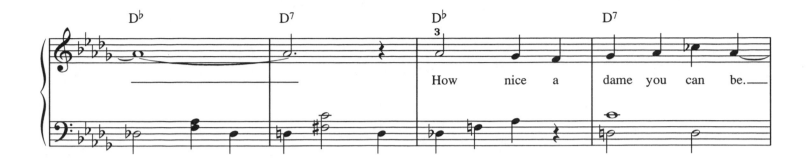

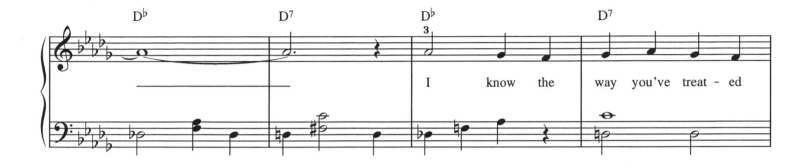

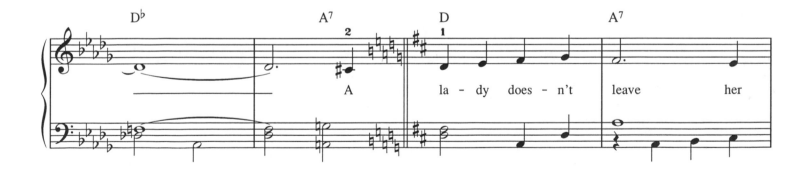

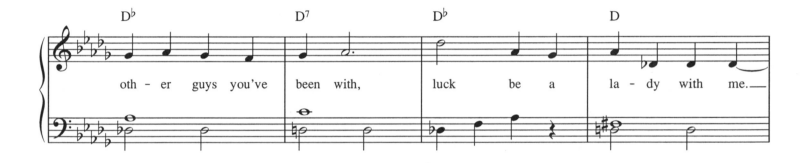

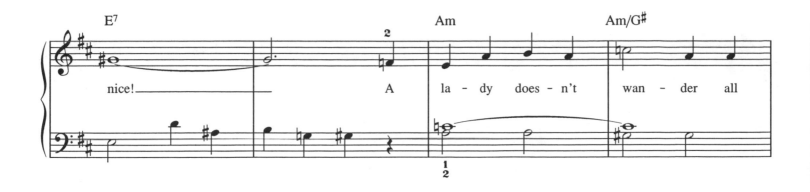

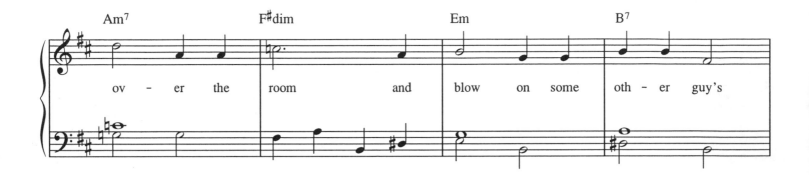

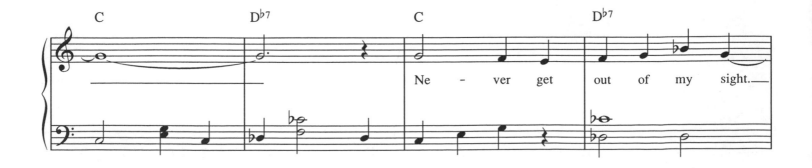

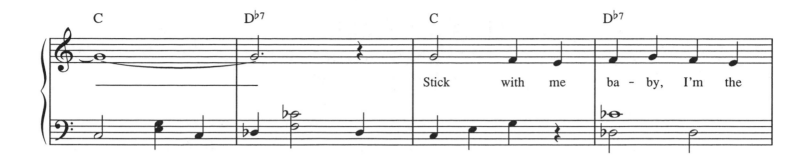

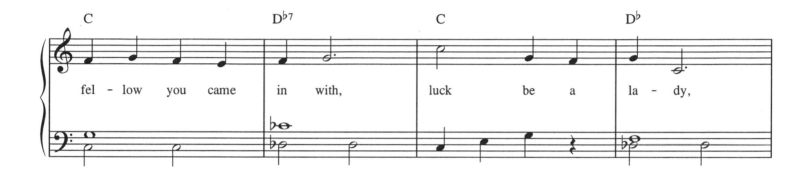

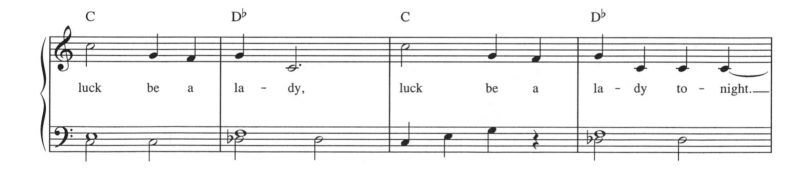

Master Of The House

(Les Misérables)

Words by Herbert Kretzmer
Music by Claude-Michel Schönberg
Original Text by Alain Boublil & Jean-Marc Natel

Moderately

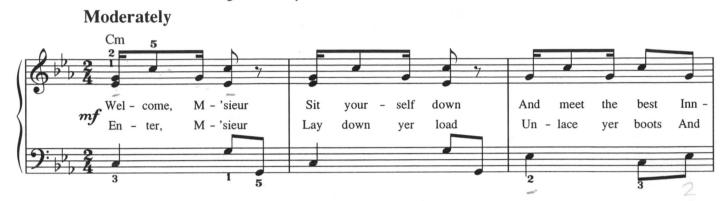

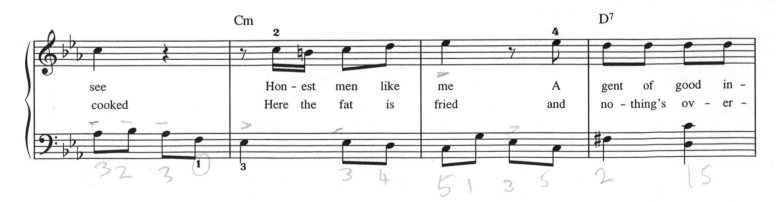

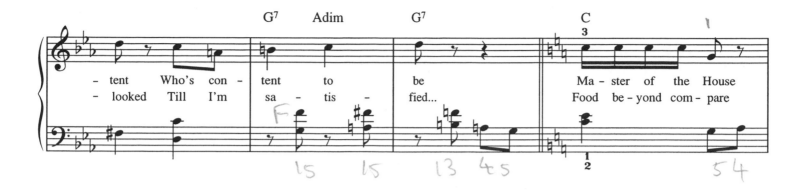

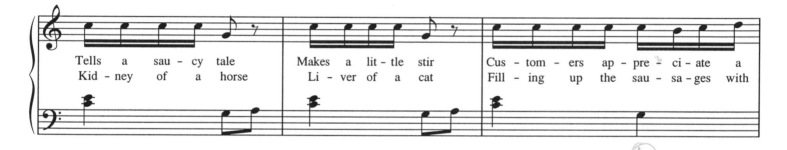

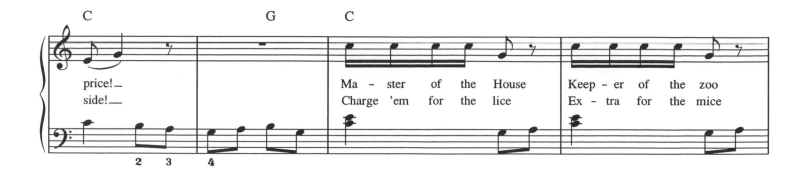

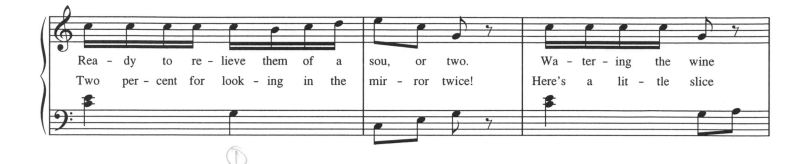

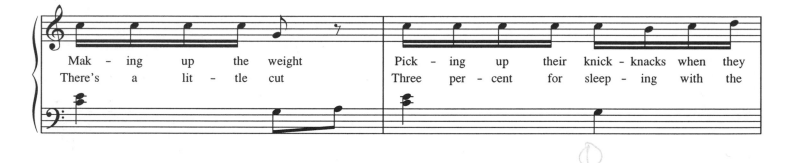

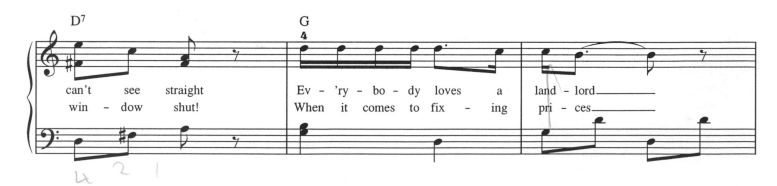

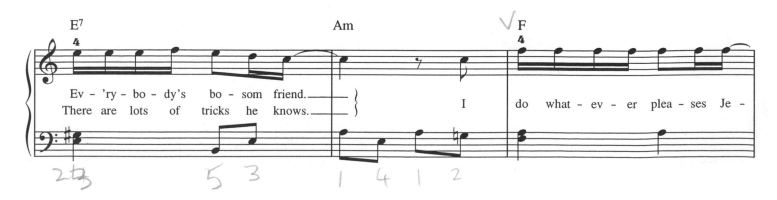

- sus! Don't I bleed 'em in the end! Ma – ster of the House Quick to catch yer eye

Ne – ver wants a pass – er by to pass him by. Ser – vant to the poor But – ler to the great

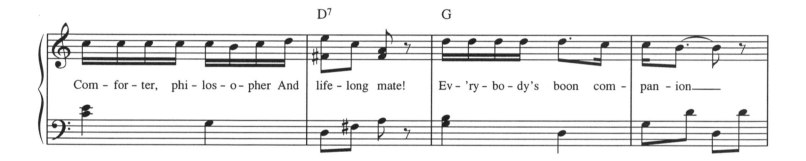

Com – for – ter, phi – los – o – pher And life – long mate! Ev – 'ry – bo – dy's boon com – pan – ion

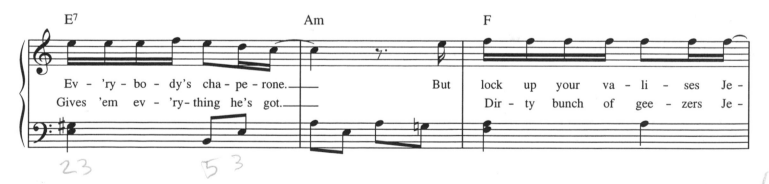

Ev – 'ry – bo – dy's cha – pe – rone. But lock up your va – li – ses Je –
Gives 'em ev – 'ry – thing he's got. Dir – ty bunch of gee – zers Je –

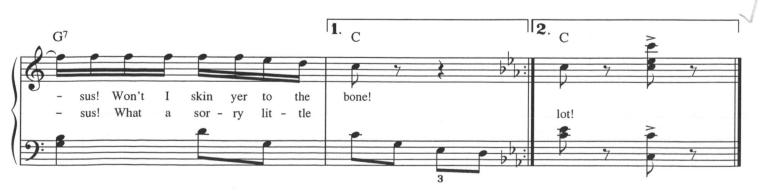

- sus! Won't I skin yer to the bone!
- sus! What a sor – ry lit – tle lot!

Me And My Girl

(Me And My Girl)

Music by Noel Gay
Words by Douglas Furber & Arthur Rose

Moderately

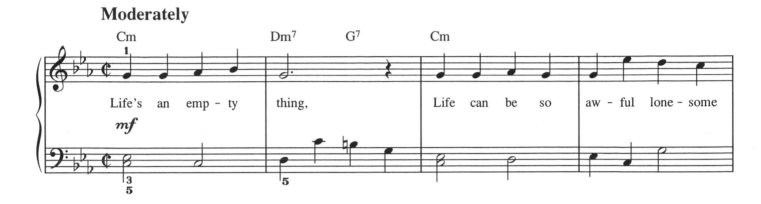

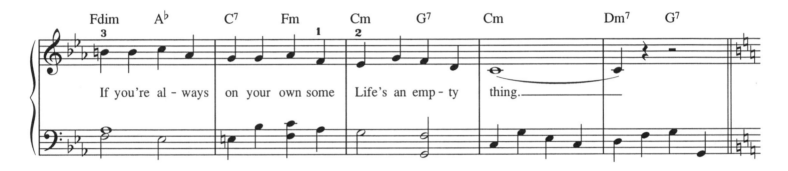

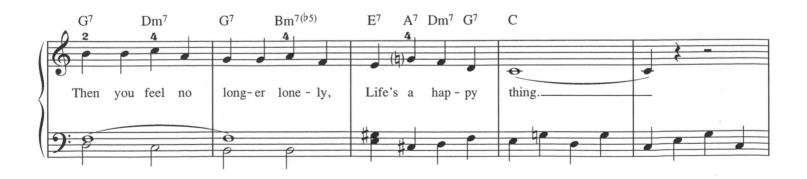

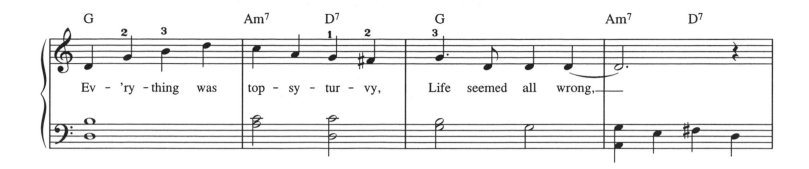

Ev - 'ry -thing was top - sy - tur - vy, Life seemed all wrong,

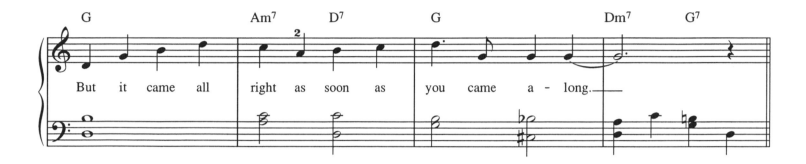

But it came all right as soon as you came a - long.

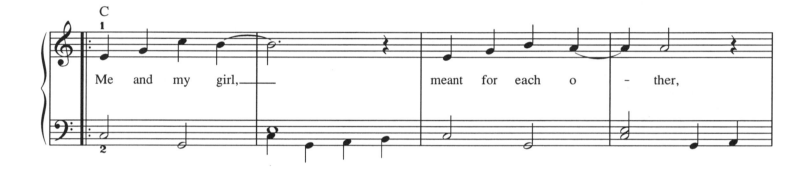

Me and my girl, meant for each o - ther,

sent for each o - ther, and lik - ing it so.

Me and my girl, S'no use pre - tend - ing,

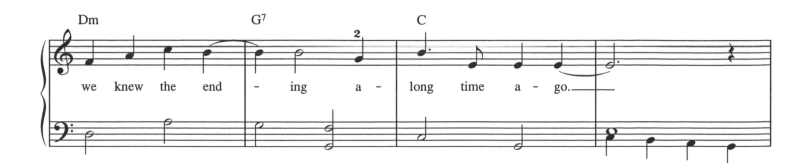

we knew the end – ing a – long time a – go.

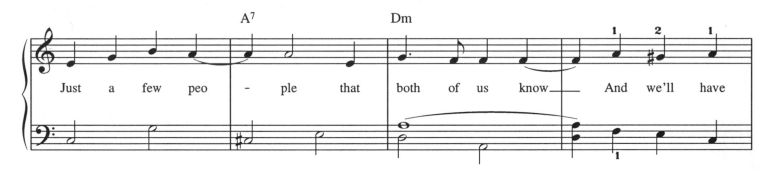

Some lit – tle church with a big stee – ple,

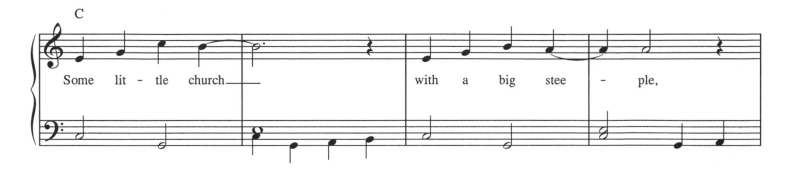

Just a few peo – ple that both of us know. And we'll have

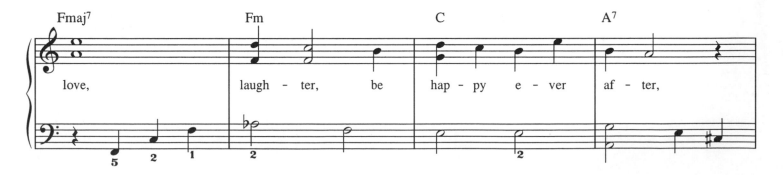

love, laugh – ter, be hap – py e – ver af – ter,

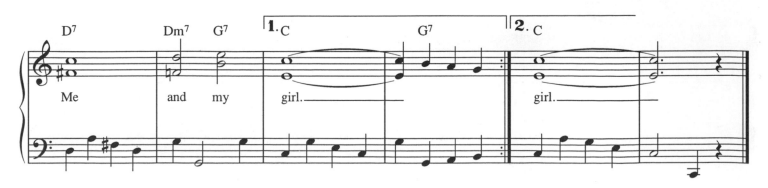

Me and my girl. girl.

Memory
(Cats)

Music by Andrew Lloyd Webber
Text by Trevor Nunn after T.S. Eliot

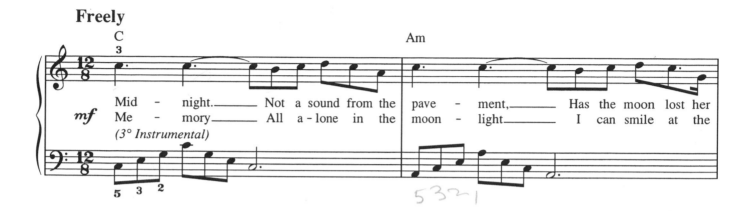

Freely

mf

Mid - night._____ Not a sound from the pave - ment,_____ Has the moon lost her
Me - mory_____ All a - lone in the moon - light_____ I can smile at the
(3° Instrumental)

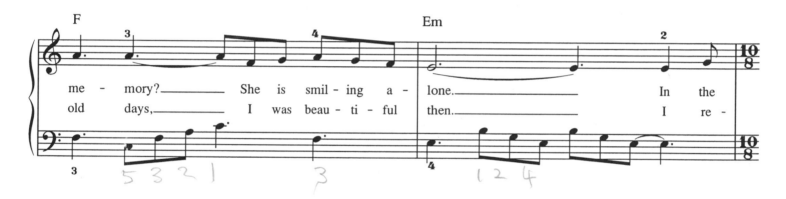

me - mory?_____ She is smil - ing a - lone._____ In the
old days,_____ I was beau - ti - ful then._____ I re -

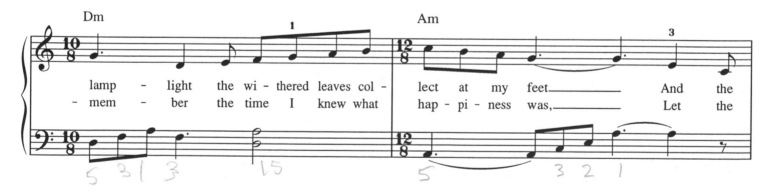

lamp - light the wi - thered leaves col - lect at my feet_____ And the
- mem - ber the time I knew what hap - pi - ness was,_____ Let the

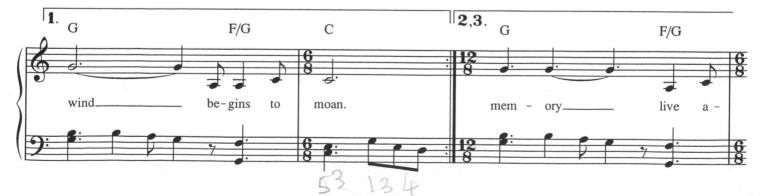

1.
wind_____ be - gins to moan.

2,3.
mem - ory_____ live a -

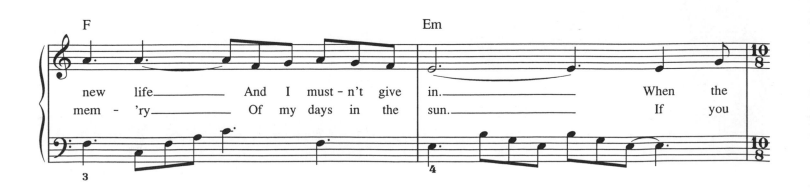

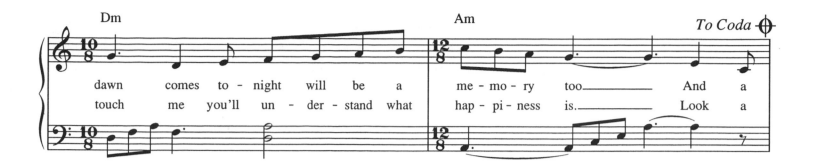

To Coda

dawn   comes   to - night will be a   me - mo - ry too   And   a
touch   me you'll un - der - stand what   hap - pi - ness is.   Look a

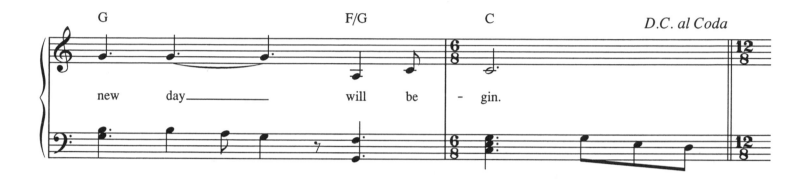

D.C. al Coda

new   day   will   be - gin.

CODA

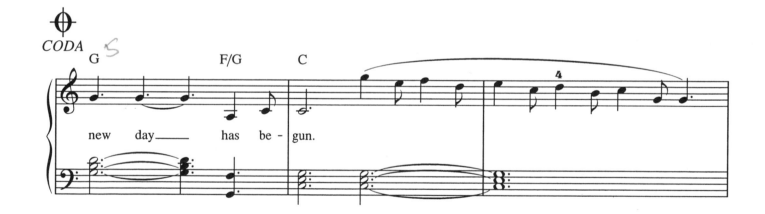

new   day   has be - gun.

pp

Ol' Man River
(Show Boat)

Music by Jerome Kern
Words by Oscar Hammerstein II

Moderately

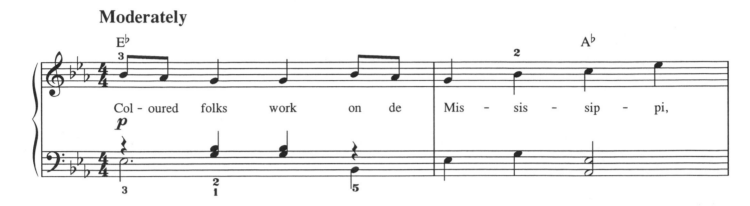

Col - oured folks work on de Mis - sis - sip - pi,

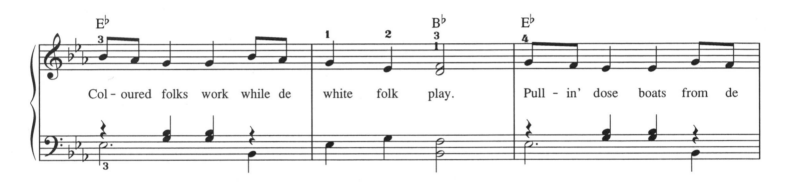

Col - oured folks work while de white folk play. Pull - in' dose boats from de

dawn to sun - set, Git - tin' no rest till de judge - ment day.

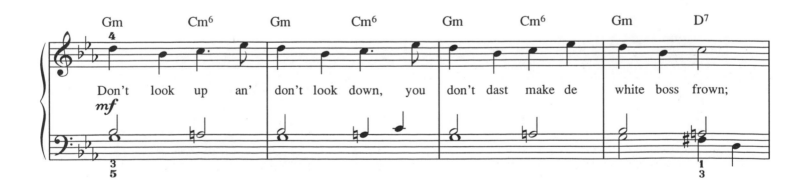

Don't look up an' don't look down, you don't dast make de white boss frown;

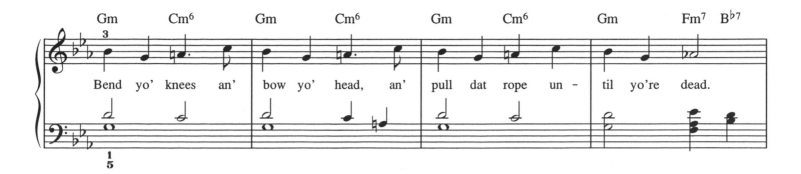

Bend yo' knees an' bow yo' head, an' pull dat rope un - til yo're dead.

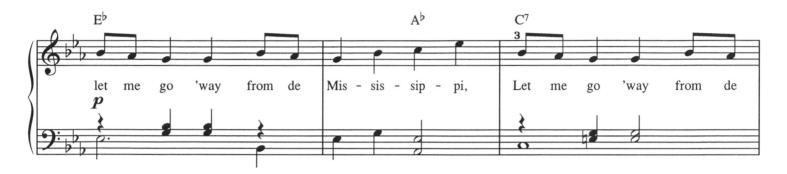

let me go 'way from de Mis - sis - sip - pi, Let me go 'way from de

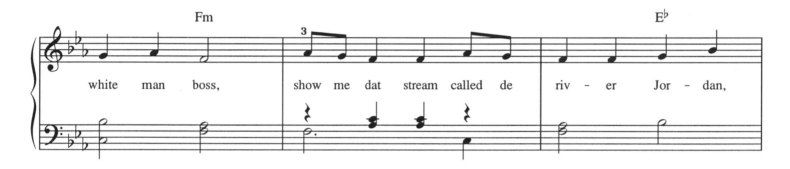

white man boss, show me dat stream called de riv - er Jor - dan,

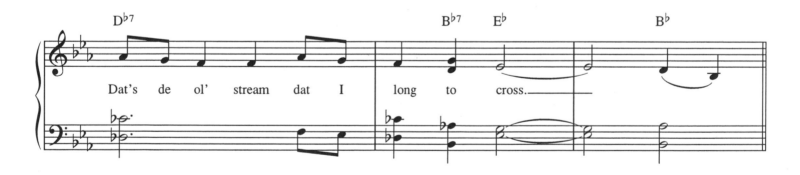

Dat's de ol' stream dat I long to cross.

Ol' man riv - er, dat ol' man riv - er, He must know sump - in', but

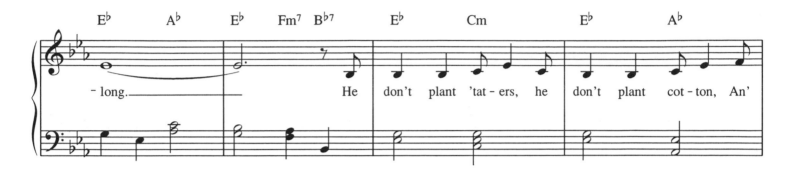

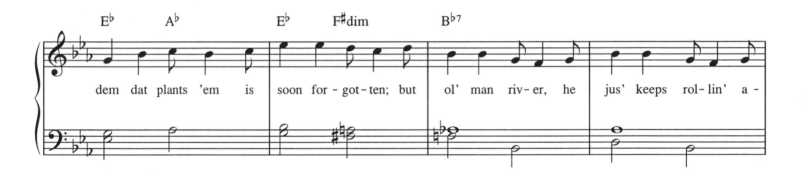

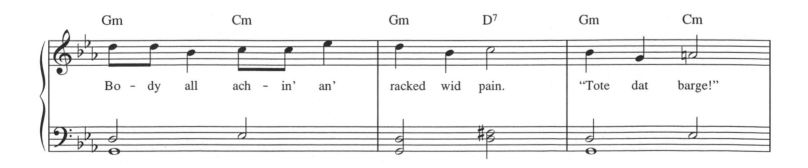

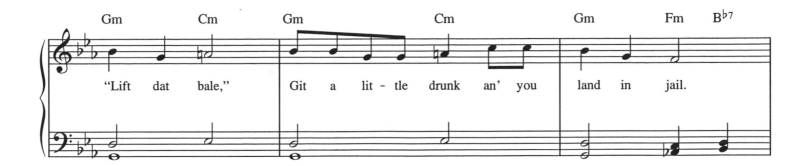

"Lift dat bale," Git a lit-tle drunk an' you land in jail.

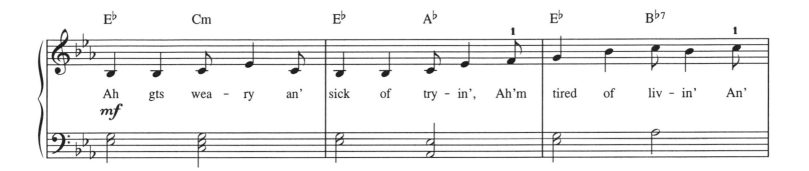

Ah gts wea-ry an' sick of try-in', Ah'm tired of liv-in' An'

mf

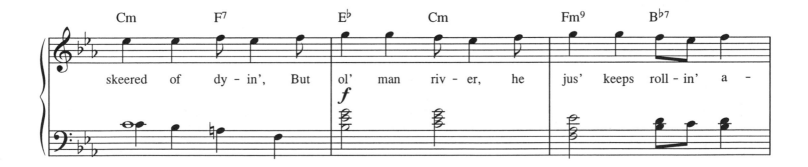

skeered of dy-in', But ol' man riv-er, he jus' keeps roll-in' a-

f

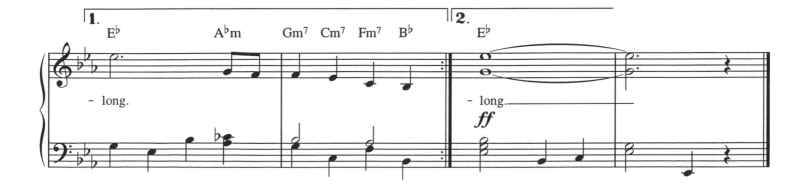

1.
- long.

2.
- long.

ff

Pick A Pocket Or Two

(Oliver!)

Words & Music by Lionel Bart

Moderately bright

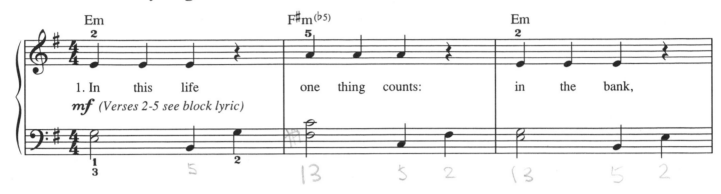

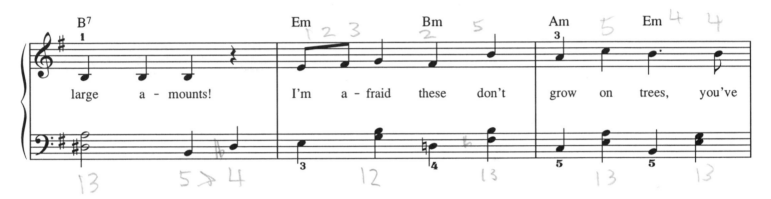

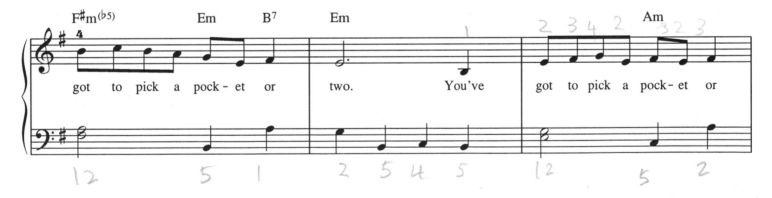

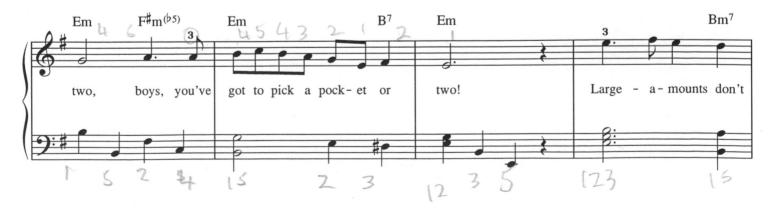

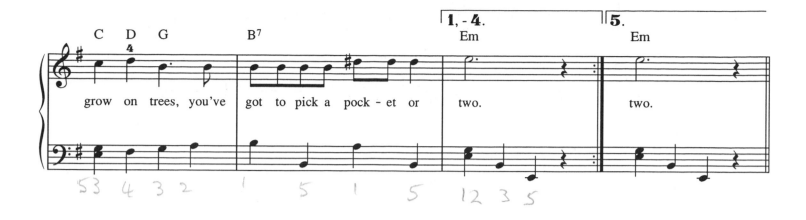

grow on trees, you've got to pick a pock - et or two. two.

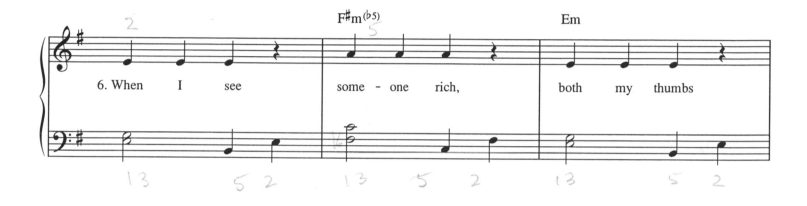

6. When I see some - one rich, both my thumbs

start to itch. On - ly to find some peace of mind. I

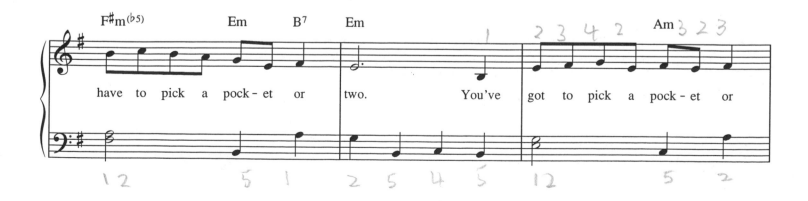

have to pick a pock - et or two. You've got to pick a pock - et or

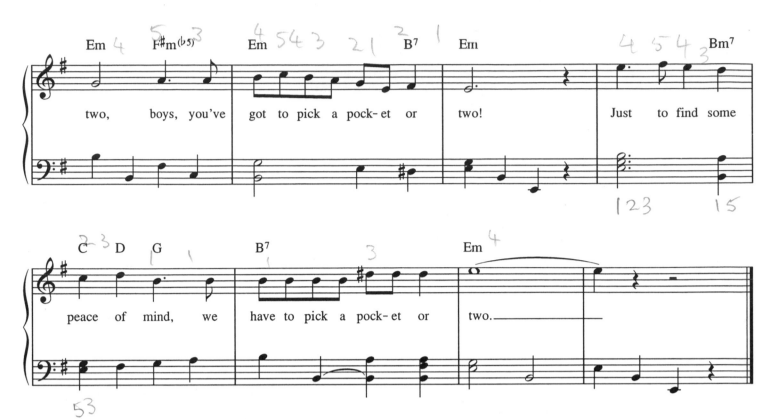

Verse 2:

Why should we break our backs, stupidly paying tax?
Better get some untaxed income: better pick a pocket or two.
You've got to pick a pocket or two, boys,
You've got to pick a pocket or two.
Why should we all break our backs? Better pick a pocket or two.

Verse 3:

Robin Hood, what a crook! Gave away what he took.
Charity's fine, subscribe to mine! Get out and pick a pocket or two.
You've got to pick a pocket or two, boys,
You've got to pick a pocket or two.
Robin Hood was far too good, get out and pick a pocket or two.

Verse 4:

Take a tip from Bill Sykes - he can whip what he likes,
I recall he started small, he had to pick a pocket or two.
You've got to pick a pocket or two, boys,
You've got to pick a pocket or two.
We can be like old Bill Sykes, if we pick a pocket or two.

Verse 5:

Dear old gent passing by, something nice takes his eye.
Everything's clear! Attack the rear! Advance and pick a pocket or two.
You've gor to pick a pocket or two, boys,
You've got to pick a pocket or two.
Have no fear, attack the rear, get in and pick a pocket or two.

Some Enchanted Evening

(South Pacific)

Words by Oscar Hammerstein II
Music by Richard Rodgers

Moderately slow

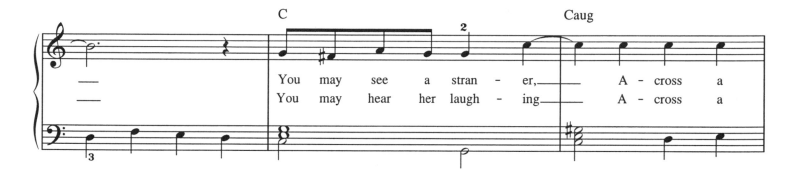

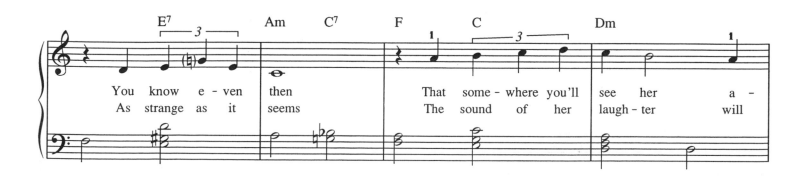

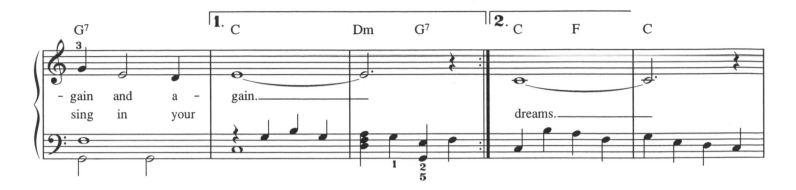

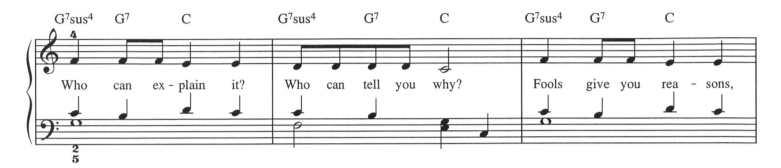

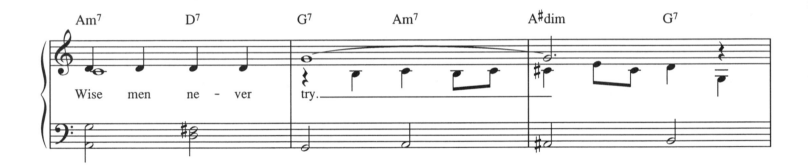

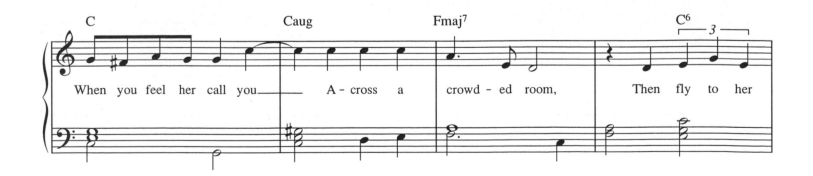

side   And make her your   own,   Or   all through your

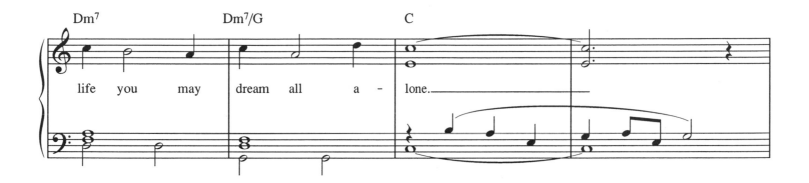

life you may   dream all   a -   lone.

Once you have found her,   Ne-ver let her go.   Once you have found   her,

Ne - ver   let   her   go!

Superstar
(Jesus Christ Superstar)

Music by Andrew Lloyd Webber
Lyrics by Tim Rice

Lively rock

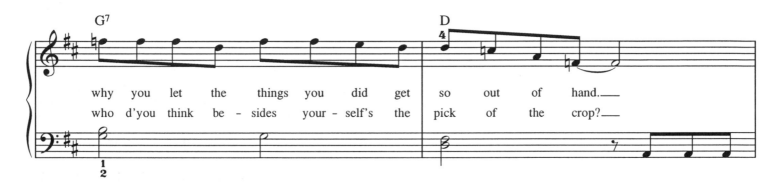

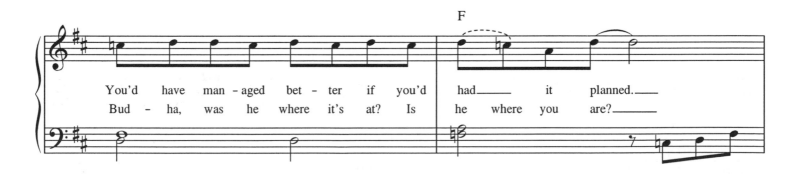

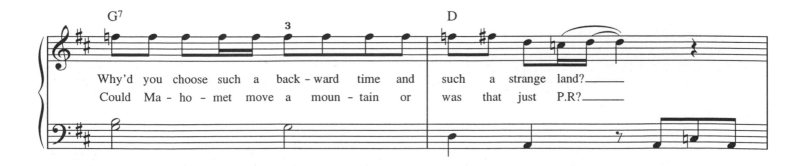

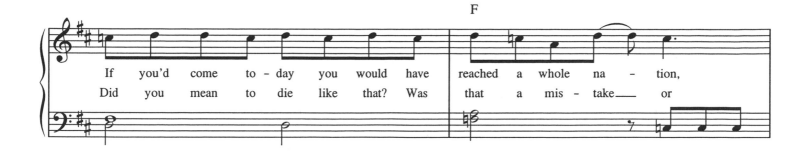

If you'd come to-day you would have reached a whole na-tion,
Did you mean to die like that? Was that a mis-take or

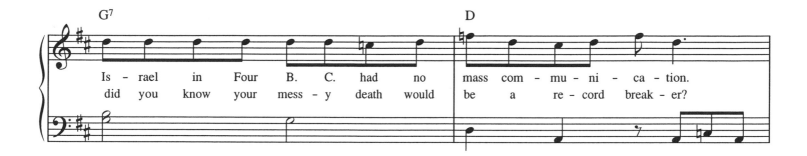

Is-rael in Four B. C. had no mass com-mu-ni-ca-tion.
did you know your mess-y death would be a re-cord break-er?

Don't you get me wrong,___   Don't you get me wrong,___   Don't you get me wrong,___

Don't you get me wrong,___   on-ly want to know,___   on-ly want to know,___

on-ly want to know,___   on-ly want to know.___

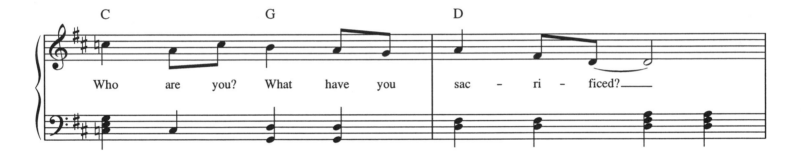

do you think you're what they say you are?—

Je - sus Christ,— su - per - star,— do you think you're what they

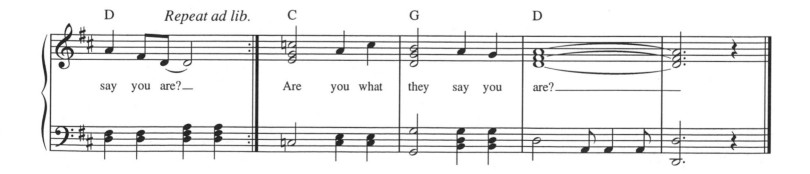

say you are?— Are you what they say you are?—————

Tonight
(West Side Story)

Words by Stephen Sondheim
Music by Leonard Bernstein

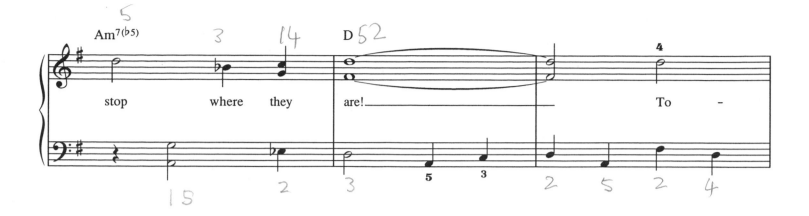

stop where they are!_____ To -

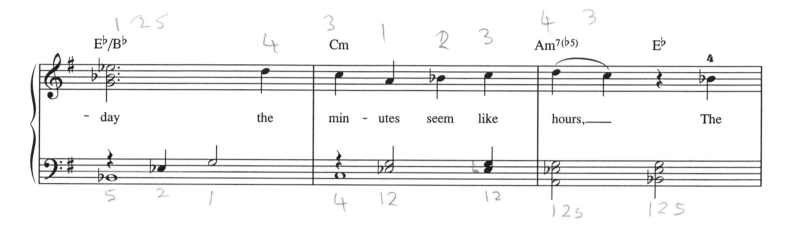

- day the min - utes seem like hours,_____ The

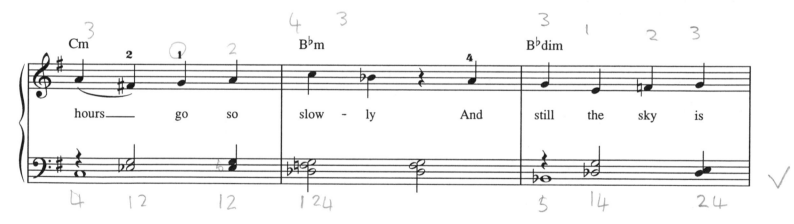

hours_____ go so slow - ly And still the sky is

light._____ O moon, grow bright, And

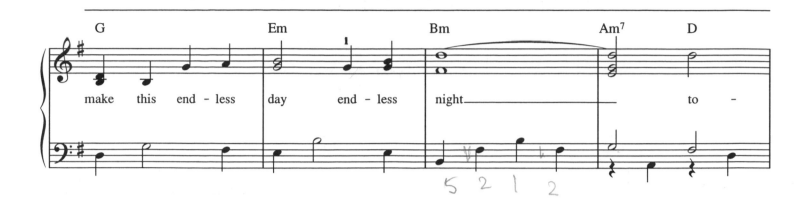

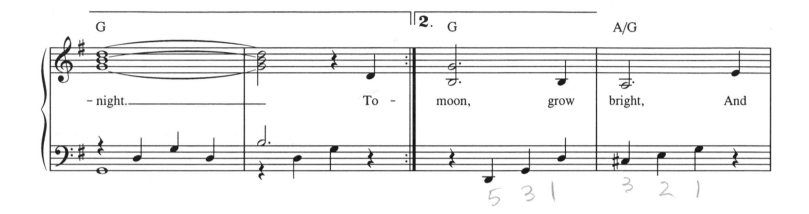

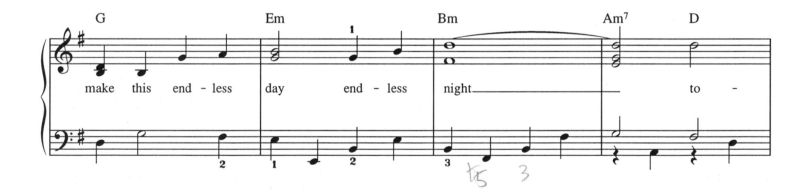

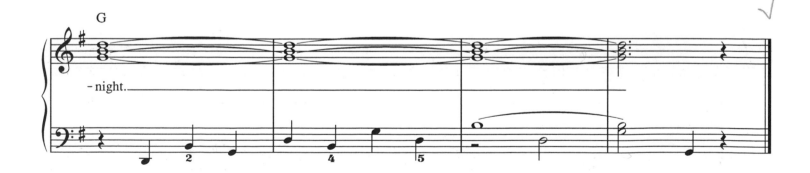

What I Did For Love
(A Chorus Line)

Words by Edward Kleban
Music by Marvin Hamlisch

Moderately

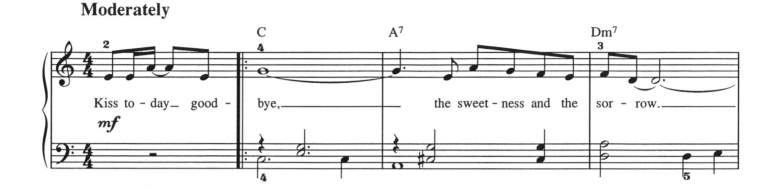

Kiss to-day_ good-bye,_____ the sweet-ness and the sor-row.____

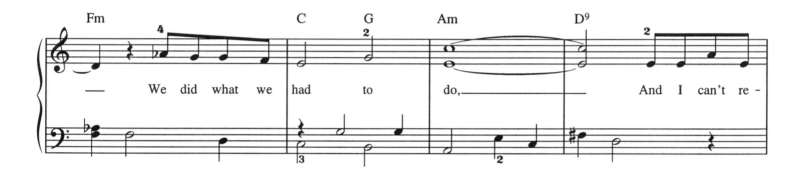

—— We did what we had to do,____ And I can't re-

-gret What I did for love, What I did for love.____ Look, my eyes_ are

dry,____ the gift was ours to bor-row.____ It's as if we

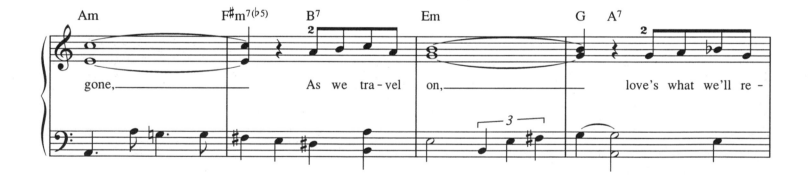

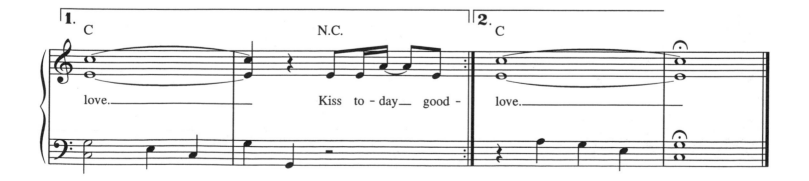

You're The One That I Want
(Grease)

Words & Music by John Farrar

Moderately

I got chills.
filled

They're mul - ti - ply - in'.
with af - fec - tion

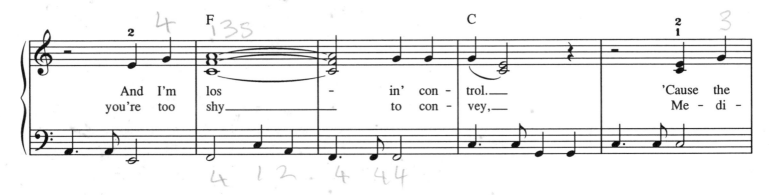

And I'm los - in' con - trol.
you're too shy to con - vey,

'Cause the
Me - di -

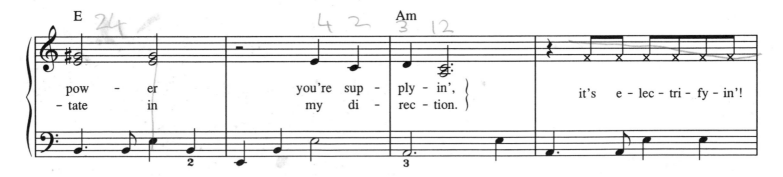

pow - er
- tate in

you're sup - ply - in',
my di - rec - tion.

it's e - lec - tri - fy - in'!

Feel your way.

I bet - ter shape
You bet - ter shape

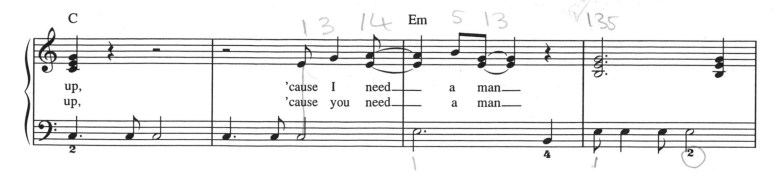

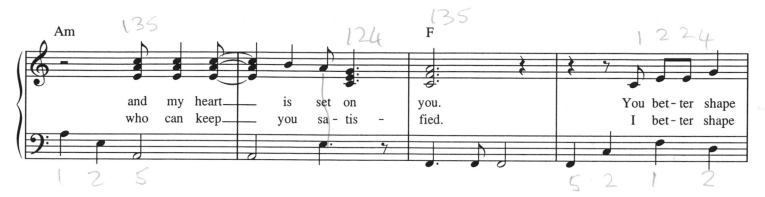

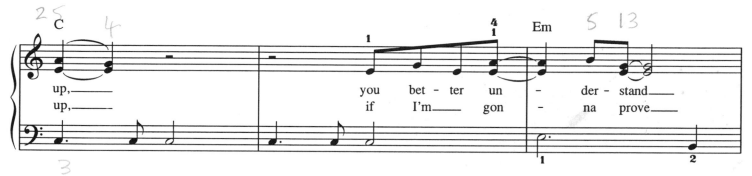

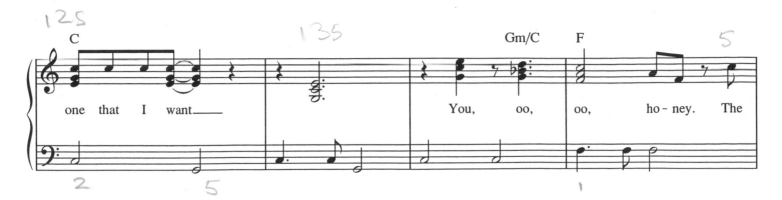

one that I want____

You, oo, oo, ho - ney. The

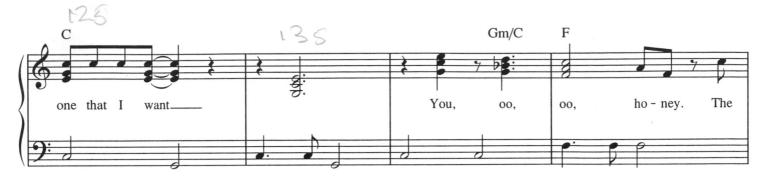

one that I want____

You, oo, oo, ho - ney. The

one that I want____

You, oo,

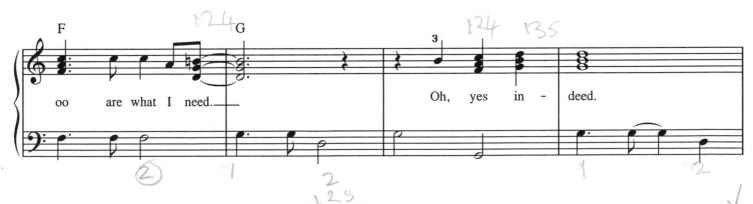

oo are what I need.____

Oh, yes in - deed.

1. If you're

2. Gsus⁴ C

You're the one that I want!____

N.C.